Convers with God

Book 1

Matthew Robert Payne

To sow into Matthew's writing ministry, to request a personal prophecy or to contact him, please visit http://personal-prophecy-today.com

This book was edited by Lisa Thompson. You can email her at writebylisa@gmail.com or visit her website at www.writebylisa.com

The opinions expressed by the author are not necessarily those of Revival Waves of Glory Books & Publishing.

Published by Revival Waves of Glory Books & Publishing
PO Box 596| Litchfield, Illinois 62056 USA
www.revivalwavesofgloryministries.com

Revival Waves of Glory Books & Publishing is committed to excellence in the publishing industry.
Book design Copyright © 2016 by Revival Waves of Glory Books & Publishing. All rights reserved.

Published in the United States of America

Paperback: 978-1-68411-043-8
Hardcover: 978-1-68411-044-5

Table of Contents

Dedication

This book is dedicated to my mother, who gave birth to me and who is my closest friend. She has seen me through some hard times, has seen me at my worst and has stayed with me and championed me to become a man of God. Everyone would be a better person if they had a mother like mine. She hopes in my future, accepts my past and supports me in the present through each decision that I make.

I want to dedicate this book to her, and I pray that every person touched by it will be credited to her rewards in heaven as a due compensation for all of the love and time that she has invested in me.

Acknowledgements

Father God

I want to thank you for taking the time to speak to me and for using this dialogue to make books that other people can read and glean from. You are a God that has our best interests at heart and not only did you minister to me through your words, but I am sure that you will touch the lives of many readers. I love to hear your heart and to know you personally and intimately. I pray that all of the people that read this book might come to know you as I do.

Lisa Thompson

I want to thank you for polishing my words and making this book a better book. You take my simple language and make it more readable and understandable. I want to thank you for working on so many books with me.

Jesus Christ

Thank you for being my Friend for all of my life. You have led me and trained me, and you have allowed me to write some good books. You are a joy to me. You introduced me to your Father, and now I am getting to know him better through these books. I am finding that he is a lot like you. While that should not come as a surprise to me, nonetheless, it did! You have helped me and led me, and I praise your holy name.

Bill Vincent

I want to thank Bill Vincent who produces my paperback books, my e-books and my audio books. His company, Revival Waves of Glory Books and Publishing, has shown me great favor, and without you, I would be spending much more money to produce books. I give you my heartfelt thanks.

The readers

I want to thank my readers. Knowing that you are going to read this book has given me the motivation to write it. My conversations with God are raw. I am used to speaking to Jesus, and so conversations with God, the Father, are something new. Knowing that you are going to read this has given me the ability to sit down 15 times and listen to what God had to say to me. I want to thank you, dear reader, for that.

What People Are Saying

Being truly open is not easy, and I applaud Matthew for being transparent with us, the readers. This book speaks from a very deep place in all of us, yet most of us don't know how to access it. Matthew has made that connection, and we can, too, but it's all up to us as seekers of our own truth to find our paths. The simplicity of the book, "Conversations with God," should show us that God is ready to communicate to us, his children, on a level that we can comprehend. This is the most wonderful aspect of being his creation that we can actually communicate with the Creator of the world! You will highly enjoy the depth and love in this book as a father/son relationship that we could all hope to have. Get ready for the realization that you, too, can have your own conversations with God after reading this book!

Dr. Colin Lieberman — www.acts29ministries.com

"Conversations with God" is a phenomenal book! "Alone" and "Imitate Jesus" are my favorite chapters. I can relate because I have been alone most of my life. Also, as Christians, we are supposed to imitate Jesus, but we don't see this in the body of Christ. I would recommend this book to anyone who doesn't believe that God speaks today. This book will show you that if we just "listen" and have faith, we can hear God speak to us. Also, God wants us to keep a journal. I love how God speaks to Matthew in this book. Very simple and not complicated. I give it 5 stars.

Lisa S. Tucker — Yahweh Place Ministry
www.yahwehplaceministry.org

Introduction

About a month ago while looking at books on Amazon, I came across one by a born-again Christian called "Conversations with God" by Suzanne D. Williams. I immediately downloaded and read it and was impressed with it. It was only a short book of about 41 pages. I was touched by the book and was happy that it was written by a Christian with biblical themes.

After I read that book, the Holy Spirit impressed upon my spirit that I was to write a book as well and call it "Conversations with God." Over the next month, I wrote 15 blogs that became this book. I followed the topics covered by my former book, "Jesus Speaking Today," where Jesus spoke to my readers. Instead of a one-page post as in "Jesus Speaking Today," the Father had a two-way conversation with me and spoke on the same subjects at length.

I am a prophet who regularly hears messages for the Body of Christ and individuals, and so the idea of sitting down and having conversations with God appealed to me. While I felt the weighty responsibility of hearing from God and recording what he was saying to people, I was also highly rewarded to hear him speak.

I was touched by what God had to say to his people, and I was impressed by the simplicity of the messages. I don't think that you need to be a Christian to understand what he said, but I can see that it would be an advantage. God didn't speak to me in profound language, yet the messages touched and impacted me. I am so glad to know a God that can explain his message in simple terms for the common folk like me.

It is my prayer that you find much that speaks to you in these messages even if you mainly see this as a dialogue between a Christian prophet and his God. Nonetheless, I pray that it will encourage you to have your own conversations with God. I hope that every reader will use this book to propel them into keeping their own journal and having a conversation with God. While you can read the conversations that others have had with God, it is much more useful for you to have your own conversations with him.

Chapter 1
Take My Hand

God:

Matthew, it is so good to start on this adventure today. I am so pleased to be here to speak to you.

Matthew:

It's awesome to think that I could sit down and speak to you and contemplate writing this book.

God:

I want you to relax. Let me take your hand and lead you in the way that we will go. You have already decided to follow the book format of "Jesus Speaking Today." You can choose topics from that book.

Matthew:

I am aware that you are going to speak to me. I am also conscious that you are going to speak to people who read this book. It's so good to sit down and contemplate having 60 or more conversations with you.

God:

Just relax, Matthew. I have been preparing you for this book for many years. I have drawn you near though my Son, Jesus. I have called you to be my prophet and a writer. This is going to be easy for you and a journal between you and me. I have been waiting all of your life for this book.

Matthew:

You are aware, God, that I have many fears, and I am not as close to you as I want to be. I pray that you will really take me by your hand and lead me. I have to admit that I am nervous speaking to you but somehow excited at the same time.

God:

Like I tell many people, Matthew, the journey of life is meant to be taken one step at a time. Whenever you are up to it, you can sit down and journal and write my words to you. I desire to be understood and to fellowship with people. I want them to sit down with me and speak to me in journals so that I can pour out my heart to them.

Matthew:

I can do this. One day at a time. One post at a time. I can work on my other books and once a day, or when I have the time, sit down and speak to you. You can walk me through this. I can keep a running dialogue with you one post at a time.

God:

Yes, today we allowed heartburn to keep you awake. You are not able to sleep, and you don't have any heartburn tablets, so I have your full attention. You'll remember one other time when we wanted you to do something important. You had heartburn, and we had you up, doing what we wanted. It's not that we gave you the heartburn, but we are happy to use your time like this.

Matthew:

I can't remember what I did the last time that I got heartburn, but yes, I know it was important. As I remember, my time with you lasted for hours that night. I stayed up the whole night and accomplished a lot with no distractions.

God:

We have such a good life for you to live. We have so much for you. Heaven is anxiously awaiting this new book, "Conversations with God," by Matthew Robert Payne. I promise that this will be a good journey for you.

Matthew:

I know that your Holy Spirit always leads me. I know that it was not a mistake that I came across that book today. Hours ago, as I tried to go to sleep, I felt your Spirit leading me to get up and start. I tried to ignore it, and yet now here we are.

God:

Yes, here we are. It is 3:33 a.m., and the three of us, the Trinity, are here with you. We will lead you and give you the words to type and the questions to ask. I will make sure that this is a great project. Everything that you do for us is good. We love to lead you and keep you on the right track. We are so proud of you. You are so easily led. I enjoy leading my people. I enjoy myself when Christians follow our lead. I enjoy walking with people hand in hand. You are so open to our Holy Spirit.

Matthew:

I don't know where I learned it from, God. It's just part of me now. I guess it is something that I learned over time. I think it came from trying to follow the commands of Jesus in everything that I did and said. I just got into a habit of listening to the Holy Spirit and doing what he said. It comes so easily for me now. Except when I try to go to sleep instead of getting up to start this book!

God:

No matter what you wanted to do, Matthew, here we are now with you, sitting on your lounge and typing my words. The words are flowing easily as we are having a good conversation. I have much to say to you through the course of these books that will come from these conversations. Yes, you heard right. We want to follow the topics of your "Jesus Speaking Today" book. Each of the conversations will be titled with the same title and in the same order as that book.

Matthew:

I feel that you make things easy for me. I feel that everything that you ask me to do can be done by me without a whole lot of effort. You make things really simple for me. I don't know why people say that you are a complex God. I know that it is impossible for men to really understand you in all of your dimensions. But I know that when it comes to me, you make things pretty simple. Thanks for being with me.

God:

I look forward to seeing you write your posts. I will enjoy getting to know you more deeply. Take care.

Chapter 2
A New Day

God:

Matthew, today I am going to do a new thing with you and the readers by faith.

Matthew:

Tell me more, God.

God:

First of all, I am going to lead you to the people that will set you free from the strongholds in your life. You already have that web address. These people will help you in a great way. I am also working to cause a shift in your life. If you trust me, I am going to do a new thing in your life, and I am going to move.

Matthew:

I am tired, Lord. I am in need of a shift. I have been feeling that things have been moving for me since Christmas when my new website went live. People have been requesting prophecies, and I have been earning good income. Money that I need to publish books is coming in. I am so happy.

God:

Yes, that is only the start. I am going to position and prepare you to start speaking in places. I am going to let certain people know who you are. I am going to work on your personal life. I am going to allow healing to come to you. I am going to build you up and get you into a place where you will be positioned to do great exploits for me. The shift starts today. Today, I am going to start things and put them in motion. People will approach you. They will read something that you have written and then make themselves known to you.

Matthew:

That sounds good. I have to admit that I have been waiting all of my life to be used. It is hard for me to believe even though you are saying it to me.

God:

Matthew, I know that it is hard for you to believe. But just as you mentioned, as your new website took effect, you have noticed things moving. Events and circumstances will increase and flow in a better way. Just as you are starting to believe in my supply for your finances, soon you will see that I can open doors. You already have the radio interview on March 13, the day before your birthday. In fact, the day will be the 13th in the USA, but when you go live from Australia, it will be on your birthday. So your website took off in December, and your first best seller took off in December, and on your birthday, you're going to be interviewed. Can you see that I am starting to move in your life?

Matthew:

Yes, it does look promising, God. It's just that I have had many things prophesied in the past that have not yet come to pass. I am a little weary of waiting. Can you understand?

God:

Yes, I know, Matthew. I understand you completely. I have also been here, waiting to do things in your life. We had a lot to do to prepare you and get you ready. You don't have to open doors. We are going before you. You will see soon that a new day is upon you. You will see the doors begin to open for you to minister. Many people like you have been waiting for years to minister who have been obedient yet have been relegated to obscurity. I am going to do a new thing in their lives. I am going to heal them, secure them and open doors for them. I am going to make a way for them after years of seemingly no way. I am going to raise up my hidden ones. I am going to allow them to shine and go forth to speak and do great things.

Matthew:

I am happy. I know what it is to be in obscurity. I know what it is like to wait for my time in the sun. Like Moses, I have waited 40 years. I am ready to be used.

God:

You are already being used, Matthew. People are buying your books and gleaning from them. Some people don't change after reading your books, but others are really affected by them, learning from them and applying them. You write good books, Matthew, and none of them are wasted. I am going to do a great thing for you — raise you up to be a leader that people know and make your name greater then you can even imagine. I am the Maker of heaven and earth. I can do great things, and my Spirit is still moving on the earth. I can make an impact when I want to make an impact. I can make your name known throughout the world.

Matthew:

A part of me is scared of being known, God. I look at my illness and my sleep issues and depression, and I wonder how I would cope if I became really popular.

God:

Matthew, you're going to take one day at a time and do one thing at a time. You are going to do things step by step. We are going to lead and heal you and equip you and hold your hand. We are going to anoint you and let you work at a pace that suits you. We are going to slowly bring you out into the light. We are going to do things in the right order and manner. As you said in the last chapter, when we have had you do something, it has always been easy. That won't change as you come into the light. We are going to pace your journey. We will always be with you and hold your hand.

Matthew:

You will be with me every step of the way, Lord?

God:

Yes, we are going to be with you. I have seen your whole future and know everything that you're going to do. I have seen all of your speaking engagements and all of the books that you write. I have seen everything. I am going to lead you in the right way. We will improve your eating habits, sleeping patterns and schedule. We will lead you at the right pace and keep you. We will prepare invitations for you to speak on what is in your heart. We will put words in your mouth. I promise you, we will hold your hand. With this new day, you're just going to get busier with each passing week.

Matthew:

It brings my heart peace when you speak to me like this. For me, I don't know my future, but you say that you have seen my whole future, and you are going to hold my hand. I am so happy that you are going to lead and direct me. I know that you have brought angels into my life. I know that they are going be with me and help me. In the past month, I have been getting to know them. They are really nice to talk to.

God:

They are there to assist you. They are like your staff. They each have a specific role to play in your life. Even as you type this, they are helping. You are doing a great work. They are going help you with many projects. They are your servants that I have appointed to you. They have each seen your whole future in heaven, and they know what they need to do to lead you and to help you with your life. I am glad that you're speaking to them and getting to know them. I wish that everyone had such a great relationship with my Son so that I could show them their angels. I wish that my people would know me and let themselves be led by me. Angels are just one part of the Kingdom that I show to people that are obedient.

Matthew:

I am excited about speaking to you each day. It has been a long time coming. I have been prophesying to people that they should journal, and now I have a journal/book that has been started with you. I am aware that you have much to teach me and share with me as I journal with you. What you have said about my life and my future has really set my heart at peace. I am sorry that I doubt sometimes when it comes to my future. I am so tired of waiting.

God:

We are tired of waiting also, Matthew. We have told the church what to do. For people who know Jesus, a whole Bible shares with them how to live a proper life. We have to wait till people are taught and told how to live their life. Not many people pick up the Bible and apply it to their lives. So many people simply go to church each week, sing a few songs and then forget the sermon. We have been waiting for the sons of God to manifest on the earth and make a change. Things are going to change for you, and you're going to have more of a voice in the coming days. You make sure to tell my people what I require of them. Be blessed.

Chapter 3
Tears in Heaven

God:

Matthew, now we start on a subject that people might not believe in.

Matthew:

Yes, Father, many people don't think that there are tears in heaven. Many people don't think that people cry in heaven, least of all, you.

God:

Yes, many people have that idea, Matthew. A day will come when there is no more sin, no more suffering and no more injustice. You only have to think about life on earth and see what normal fathers go though. When a child suffers on earth, the eyes of their mother and father fill with tears. On earth when people suffer, other people become emotional. Amazingly, people assume that in some way, I am less than an earthly father. If I am a God of love and I consist of love, how does it make sense that I am not affected by the sufferings of people on earth?

Matthew:

I know, right? I assume that people have Revelation 21:4 in mind that says that you will wipe every tear from people's eyes. I guess they think that this verse applies only to heaven now and not to the future.

God:

People have many beliefs because they don't fully understand scripture. Many people suffer when the Bible is not taught properly. Some of them have heard this teaching and assume that I really don't care for them.

Matthew:

I know. It must hurt people when they think that you are oblivious to their suffering.

God:

It breaks my heart that people assume that. I hurt when people suffer, yet it breaks my heart even more that people teach that I don't care about them. I see the suffering of every single person on earth. I don't just see the suffering of Christians or only hear their prayers. I hear every cry for help, and I wish that the Christians in the world could provide answers for every suffering person. Even when people did not believe that he was the Messiah, my Son still acted in love. He healed every person that came to him for help. I wish that the church would act and relieve the suffering in this broken world.

Matthew:

How do you cope with that?

God:

It's hard, Matthew. It's hard to have a Son that came to earth and taught people how to live a Christian life, yet people who are in church for years have no idea what my Son taught. It is hard to watch people suffer and harder still to see a Christian not doing anything to stop suffering when they could. All of these things and more are hard on me. I cry for the people on the earth. I am God and the Creator of all things, but it saddens me to see the world and what could be done if people knew the truth and practiced what my Son taught. It's hard. I need my prophets to speak. I need people to make a noise. I need people to teach my people. So much more could be done that is not being done.

Matthew:

How do you think that people can change?

God:

People need to understand that everyone matters to me. People need to understand that you can say that you love me with all your heart, but if you do not love your brother and sister with real needs who is right in front of you, then your words about loving me are empty. People need to rise up and take action. People need to be little Christs everywhere that they go. People need to open their eyes to the needs all around them and address those needs. People need to stop playing at church and at the Christian life, and they need to start to follow Jesus and be Jesus to everyone that they meet.

Matthew:

This really burdens your heart, doesn't it? I can really feel your heart. How will the world change? How will people make the needed changes?

God:

Yes, this burdens my heart, Matthew. I long for a people that don't just call Jesus Lord and Savior but act and walk like Jesus did in everything that they say and do. I think that we need a lot of people to start to modeling Christ and teaching people how to act like him. I need prophets that love the people to model proper living. I need people that not only model Christ but who teach others how to do it. I need a generation of people to change. I need a revolutionary group of people to say and do what needs to be done.

Matthew:

These things are really important to you.

God:

Yes, they are important to me. You live on an earth with challenging circumstances. People are turning away from the institutional church because they see it lacks authenticity, power and the love of Christ. We need a church that is a Body and that works together with itself. Every denomination needs to see the other denominations as brothers and sisters. Churches need to come together in cities and take the love and answers of Christ into the needs of their city. It really helps to speak my mind. So many people don't allow me to speak. People have their ideas of what is right doctrine and beliefs and don't accept anything that does not agree with what they believe.

Matthew:

I did not know that you got frustrated, but it must get you down, God.

God:

You have a false belief about that. People assume that because I am God and in charge of everything that I could not grow frustrated. I am frustrated with the world. Don't get me wrong. The average Christian does not know that they could be doing better. The average believer thinks that going to church each week, reading their Bible and praying makes them a good Christian. They are good people, but they do not know that we need their help to make the world a better place. Many Christians have no idea how to change the world where they live. They know about suffering but feel powerless to fix it. I understand that. I know that they don't know. But as the prophet declared, "without knowledge, my people perish."

Matthew:

How can they learn what they don't know?

God:

I need to raise up people to teach them. I need to raise up people like you to have a voice. I need to raise up prophets and teachers that don't have an agenda to be popular. I have to raise up a group of people that are willing to be radical. I need my mavericks. I need people to learn the truth, live the truth and then teach the truth to my people. I need to make changes in the church. I need to make a way for unknown people to have a voice. I need to encourage my servants that know the truth to walk by faith and walk through the doors that I open for them to preach. I need people like you.

Matthew:

This is exciting, yet we have so many teachers and preachers in the world. I wish that they were teaching people the truth. I wish that you didn't cry in heaven. I wish that the world was going better. It seems a shame that we have so many teachers in the world, but we still need more. Speaking to you shows me a little of what you are going through up there. I know that I am just one voice and just one teacher, but I won't be ashamed to teach the people what you tell me to teach them.

God:

Matthew, it does my heart well to talk to you. You are my friend. I look forward to speaking to you more as we produce these books. Be blessed!

Chapter 4
The Daily Grind

God:

Life is complex, Matthew. There is more to life than meets the eye as the cliché says. As God, I want to be with you during the good times and the bad. I want to be with people when everything is going well and especially when things are not going so well. Life can sometimes overwhelm you, and people can easily fall into the daily grind day after day.

Matthew:

As you know, Father, I struggle with a mental illness. Sometimes, I am overwhelmed with depression. At those times, I find it hard to even get out of bed and eat. I am sure that many of my readers struggle with various difficulties. My life can be a challenge.

God:

Life can be hard, Matthew. You are not a Christian in a vacuum. The life and death of my Son, Jesus, was meant to shine a light into all of your days. I know that you live with depression and as of yet, you haven't been healed, but I want you to draw strength in the knowledge that Jesus was a man of sorrows. Christ should not just be a man in a book to the church, but he should be your source and your friend. I know that Jesus is indeed your friend, and even in your most depressed states, you still connect with him. I wish it were so for every person on earth. I wish that they knew Jesus like you do and that they knew that his past life on earth and current life in heaven hold all the keys for a successful life on earth.

Matthew:

I do know Jesus fairly well. I have been talking back and forth with him for years now. I do find great comfort in having revelation about his life on earth. I share a lot about that in my two books, "Finding Intimacy with Jesus Made Simple" and "Jesus Speaking Today." I was so blessed that your Holy Spirit gave me such good revelation into the life of Jesus in those two books. Sometimes, I wish that I could give those books away and that the whole world could read them. I agree that the keys to life can be found in the person of Jesus Christ, both in the knowledge of his past life on earth and in a relationship with him in heaven right now. It does my heart good to know that he was a man of sorrows as Isaiah prophesied. It also does my heart good to know that he was rejected and misunderstood by his peers. I find so much comfort in knowing Jesus. He really is the way, the truth and the life. My life really has no purpose outside of him.

God:

We are having you write these books because of this, Matthew. You have spent many years getting to know Jesus and being led by the Holy Spirit. Indeed, you grew to know who I am through Jesus. No one can come to me except they come through the living door of Jesus. He is more than some historical person that lived a holy life and was killed by the Jews and the Romans. He is the way. In him, the world is held together. In him, life makes sense. In him, people find the answers to their struggles on earth. Spending your time getting to know Jesus is the best investment that you could make. I like to rave about my Son, Jesus. I like to lift up his Name. He is the righteous King of Kings. I spend time speaking to you, not only to draw close to you, but so that your readers, no matter how many, are blessed.

Matthew:

I've read some books where people wrote they spoke to you, which made me hungry for more of you. Little did I know that one day, I would sit at my computer and type while you spoke to me. Little did I know in those years that I would ever be a writer in my own right. Now today, I am amazed by what has happened. I see the love that you have for your Son. I see the honor that you give him. I see and hear that you agree that he is the way, the truth and the life. It warms my heart to hear you speak with so much affection about the Darling of Heaven. Jesus is my life. He is the breath that I breathe. He is the answer to my life. My whole purpose is found in him. He allows me to cope with my life. Knowing him is everything to me.

God:

I really wish that everyone would come to know Jesus like you do, Matthew. Life on earth would be a whole lot better if people really knew him and if they could act like he did on earth. Oh, what a joy it would be if people were like him instead of just wearing his name. My Son said, "Why do you call me Lord, Lord and do not do what I say?" (Luke 6:46). The same could be said today. So many people sing to Jesus and tell you that they love him, but they do not devote their whole lives to him and what he taught. Jesus said that a fool builds his life on the sand (Matthew 7:26). He said that if you hear what he taught but don't do what he says, you are building your life on the sand. I am concerned that people claim to be followers of Jesus, yet their lives are nothing like his. I am concerned for the church and organized religion. They are more interested in keeping up appearances than in preaching and walking in truth. That will change, though.

Matthew:

My heart aches for you, Father. You are speaking like your words are going forth, but no one is listening.

God:

People want to find meaning in life. They want to get off the merry-go-round and stop the drudgery of the daily grind. But they cannot see that abiding with my Son, the vine, is the only way to have a meaningful life and to have an existence that counts for anything. I speak so much about my Son and what he taught because this is the key to life and peace. In his wisdom is the wisdom of the ages. My Son came and shared the answers to successful living, and rather than preaching his commands and sharing what he taught, people just seem to preach and play religion. So much blindness is present in my church. People are blind and are often led by blind guides. The church is declining because many people cannot stomach religion and empty rules and regulations. The church needs to rise up and walk just as Jesus walked. The true apostles and prophets must arise and lead my people into the promised land of freedom, power and provision. A new age is upon us.

Matthew:

I am amazed to hear you speak. You sound just like Jesus and the Holy Spirit. You speak right to my heart. I wish that millions of people could read this. The church really needs to hear this.

God:

I love my church. I don't want people to get the wrong idea about what I am saying. The church, in many respects, is doing a fine job. Many passionate Christians know my Son's commands and walk in them. Many people are awake and are not blind to the truth, but for the large part, they are maligned and misunderstood like my Son was. Truth exists as clear as day in the Bible, but much of the church has been blinded by the god of this world similar to the way that the Jews have a veil over their eyes. I want people to wake up and not only focus on what Jesus taught but start to abide in him and do everything he taught. I want my Church to walk hand in hand with Jesus through their week and not just sing songs about him on Sunday.

Matthew:

I feel your heart. I am with you.

God:

I have so much for you, dear reader. I want you to know my Son. I want you to know who he was when he was on earth. I want you to know him now and have a conversational relationship with him. I want you to go to your Bible and highlight everything that he said to do and not to do. I want you to start to obey what he taught with the power of the Holy Spirit working through you. I want you to be a little Jesus and walk with him. We have no time for one-day-a-week Christianity. The people of the world need you, and the world needs answers and help. We don't have time to waste but must follow in the footsteps of Christ. It's time. Each of us must become anointed ones. We must all shine like the stars in the heavens. It's time. We must prosper and help others prosper. It's time. We must leave the daily grind behind and start to live life with purpose and meaning! Be blessed.

Chapter 5
Hope Floats

God:

Hello, Matthew. How are you doing today?

Matthew:

I am a bit nervous, God. It is a big responsibility to carry your words to the readers. Sometimes, it weighs on me.

God:

It is supposed to weigh on you and make you nervous. If you didn't feel a weight or a little nervousness; well, it might be coming from your flesh and not from me. You can relax as you have heard from me and my Son thousands of times. If I have nothing to say, then you simply won't hear me speak. Just like yesterday, you did not feel in the mood to type, so we didn't bring you a word to give. I am with you through all of this. I have a lot to say to the people, but you're the vessel that I am going to use, so you have to be reasonably comfortable to be the person that brings the message. I don't force myself on anyone. So it is good to feel the weight, the burden of bringing a word, and it is good to be a little nervous because carrying my words brings responsibility.

Matthew:

You are going to speak about hope today?

God:

Yes, hope is very important in this life. Many people that take their own life do so because they have run out of hope for living. The problems that they face outweigh the hope that they have in life.

Matthew:

That is so sad. I have been there.

God:

Yes, you have been there. Each time you were about to kill yourself, we sent someone along to give you a fresh burst of hope so that you could go on living. We almost lost you a few times. Look at all of the hundreds of people that are being blessed by your books these days. None of them would have been blessed and taught things if you had taken your life. Because you have suffered and gone through some hard experiences, your voice carries authority. With that authority, we are able to lead and teach people important lessons. You have finally found hope for living. When we showed you 50 books in heaven that you will write in your life, hope began to spring up in you about your purpose and your usefulness. Hope floats in your life now.

Matthew:

Yes, that is so true. I have so much hope now, knowing that I am going to write 50 books. It has had a remarkable effect on my life. I am busy every day, working hard to make that a reality. Even this conversation that I am having with you is becoming a book. You are perfect and wise. With that one vision of 50 books that I had in heaven, hope sprung up in my heart, and I have never been the same since. I am so honored that you would consider me to have so much to say to your people. I feel so blessed and happy. Even when depression hits, I am able to cope because I have this hope in my future.

God:

I would love to show every person why they are here. I personally know how much joy a person lives in when they know why they are here. People need to know their purpose, have dreams and a way to pursue their dreams. A life without purpose or meaning has no direction. It can easily become a daily grind for those people. I am a God of endless possibilities and joy. People seem to think that I am a God that expects people not to sin and mess up and nothing more. But I am a God that has plans for people, plans to give them a bright future and a precious hope in living, as it says in Jeremiah 29:11. I am the God of opportunity, adventure and purpose. It is never my intention for people to live a life without achieving their destiny and purpose. The sad fact is that not many people teach on purpose and destiny, and therefore, few people understand how to find meaning for their life.

Matthew:

I know how hard it is when you don't have purpose. I know what is is like to have no direction and no hope. I don't wish that for anyone.

God:

The fact is that you are only human, Matthew. You are not me. Though sometimes you can sense my heart and emotions, you don't feel them with the intensity that I have. I am the Creator and the Father of all men. I am the Architect and desire all people to find their purpose. A person who does not know their purpose and the reason why I created them is a person whose life is being wasted on earth. My heart breaks. It is just like a father and mother on earth seeing a child of theirs unemployed and doing drugs all of his life. If their child never received an education and never was motivated to get a job, it would break their hearts. If a parent brought up a child with love and care, and the child became a person with no motivation or interest in working or having a purpose and lived with the same kind of aimless people who spent their days drinking and doing drugs, then this would break a parent's heart.

Matthew:

Yes, that would concern a parent.

God:

I am not saying that if you have no direction or purpose that you're like an unemployed person doing drugs. I am simply trying to make you see how I feel about you when you don't have purpose or a sense of destiny. Your life is a waste. When I create people, I create them to have a clear reason for their life with tasks that I want them to do. And just like parents, it breaks my heart to see people without hope and direction in life. Conversely, when a person has an idea of what they want to do in life and starts to walk in their destiny day by day and decision by decision, this makes my heart glow. I am so happy for them and for the people their life will influence. This book is the same way to me.

Each day, you sit down with no words and listen to me, and we fill the pages together. I am so excited for the people that are going to read this and learn about me and what I desire. I am so happy that you are being led by my Holy Spirit and the angels and even by your own decision to sit down each day to write this book. I know that my words are blessing you and will positively affect those who read them. I have something for everyone to do — a purpose for them. They simply have to work out what they want to do with their lives.

Matthew:

Yes, it makes a real difference to know what you're here for and to be busy doing it.

God:

One way to discover your purpose is this. Think to yourself, "If I entered the lottery and won $10 million, enough to live the rest of my life in comfort, what would I do?" Think about it, reader. What would you do if that were you and all of your living expenses were covered for the rest of your life? What is it that you have always wanted to do? Is there something you want to be — an artist or a writer or a chef? What would you love to do with your life? When you can answer that, you need to make plans to do that job or activity. Unless you find a way to do that, you won't ever have a life of satisfaction and purpose. Your purpose is found in your dreams. You have to make plans and find a way to work towards and achieve your dreams, or you will always live a life that is second rate.

Matthew:

It may be hard for people to change careers. They have bills and commitments.

God:

Bills and commitments are simply a part of life. For example, if you want to be a writer, you don't have to write full time and earn your whole income from writing, especially to start. But you do need to begin writing and write your first blog post or your first book. You can only perfect something that you begin to do. No one becomes very good at something without practice. You will never become a great writer if you never attempt to write. You need to find a book or a person to teach you how to write, and then you need to set time aside and write. The more you write, the better you will become. And soon enough, your life will be full of hope and purpose, and your hope will help you float above the worries and concerns that are found in life. Be blessed.

Chapter 6
Fresh Thoughts

God:

Hello, Matthew, today we are going to have a good time.

Matthew:

Really? This sounds like a subject that has a lot of potential.

God:

Yes, it does. I am going to lead people this year into a new way of thinking. I am going to work in them to renew their minds. I am going to use many vehicles to speak to them. If they are readers, I am going to use books that I lead them to and retrain their minds. If they like videos, I am going to let them come across videos that are going to teach them things that I want them to learn. Do you know how YouTube suggests videos on the side that are related to the video that you are watching?

Matthew:

Yes, Lord. I know those.

God:

Well, this year, I am going to have my Holy Spirit bring up videos on the side that are meant to train my people with things I want them to know. People will start with a video they want to watch, and my Holy Spirit will lead them on a journey and discovery of what we want them to watch. We are going to lead people and educate them the way that we want to. The same goes for books. In the section on Amazon that says, "Customers who bought this item also bought," we will advertise books that we want individuals to read. We will lead our people to the new ideas and fresh thoughts that we want them to have.

Matthew:

That is really funny because this has already been happening with me. I often look at the suggested videos and buy the suggested books. I didn't fully realize that your Holy Spirit was leading me. Of course, some of the suggested videos are garbage, but I see your point. I will be more aware of it this year going forward. I pray that it will also be so for the readers.

God:

You don't have to pray that it will be so for the readers, Matthew. I will make it so. We will teach and lead our people and help them see the truth. We will change the hearts of the people that we love. We will hold the right hand of our people and lead them where we want to take them.

We are going to educate our loved ones and our church. Some of the people we want to educate saw this book that way and bought it, and now, they are reading this. They saw this advertised on another Amazon book page, and my Holy Spirit led them to it. And here they are reading.

Matthew:

This is exciting, Lord. I have always thought that you were with me, leading me, but it helps for you to say this plainly to me here and now. I ask that you continue to lead me.

God:

We are going to lead you and the people. Our angels can work with the algorithms of Amazon and YouTube and bring up any selection that we want to bring up. My Holy Spirit can guide your eyes to the suggestion and give you the desire to click on it. We also guide the writer as to what to write, and we guide the video producer about what to say and display. We can do much in the process of getting you and your readers educated in the ways that we want you educated. We can even lead a friend of yours to read a book that we want you to read and then inspire them to post a link to the book on Facebook so that you see the book. We are working in many ways behind the scenes.

Matthew:

It is really cool to talk to you. So you are saying that many good books that I have read were not just my own random choices but choices your Holy Spirit made for me?

God:

Yes, that is true. We even lead you to be in the right mood to read a certain chapter. We position you in the right way so that you can best receive from the book that you choose. We might have had a video teach you something the day before and then, when you pick up the book, it continues on the theme of the video, adding to it. We have no end to the ways that we work all things together to benefit you. We know what is ahead of you for your whole life, and we are constantly working on giving you fresh thoughts and ideas to better prepare you for the future that you are facing and the job that we have for you to do here on earth.

Matthew:

You seem to have everything solved.

God:

Well, man still has free will. We might lead you to a book, and the author might say something that you don't agree with, so you might put down the book. You need to be teachable and not offended when someone says something that you don't agree with. Instead, keep reading. My Holy Spirit and your angels try to get you to keep reading, but sometimes, you are even too stubborn to follow our leading.

Sometimes, the lesson that we want you to find is lost to you because you don't keep reading. Sometimes, we can lead you to read the book at another time when you are going through your Kindle books; sometimes, we can't get you to reread the book. At these times, we might lead you to another book that says the same thing that we want you to know. We are vigilant in your life to train and educate you how we want you to be. What you think are your choices and your research might simply be you being led by us.

Matthew:

You are funny. It is so exciting to know that you're leading me. I feel so much better now. I am excited.

God:

Yes. Sometimes, the book that we lead a person to is one of your books, Matthew. Sometimes, we let a person find one of your books, and they enjoy it, and we lead them to look at other books that you wrote. They might start with a book that they think is

41

going to educate them and read it, but we might want them to read another book of yours. When they read your first book, they find that they like you as an author, and they search for other books by you.

The second or the third book that they read of yours might be the one that we are leading them to.

It works the same with you. You find a book you like on a subject you like by a certain author, and you read it. Then, you look for other books by the author, and suddenly, you are reading a book that we wanted you to read. I want to tell you that even though we wanted you to ultimately read the second or third book, you didn't waste your time or information from what you learned in the other books that led you to it. We use everything in your life, even false teaching, to better mold you into who we want you to be.

Matthew:

So nothing is wasted?

God:

Yes, your favorite verse applies here. "All things work together for good for those that love God and are called according to His purpose" (Romans 8:28). I use everything in your life — every true and even false teaching — to shape and mold you into the person that I want you to be. I am excited to explain this to you. In my world, this is foundational information, not rocket science. But I can see that it is new revelation to you.

Matthew:

Yes, it is simple but fascinating. Some people are afraid of being deceived and taught wrong things, yet you are saying even if we are deceived, you make sure it works out for our good anyway?

God:

Exactly!

Matthew:

That is so liberating. That gives me so much more freedom. That is just so encouraging. I need not worry then. I should just read and watch whatever I set my heart to without concerns?

God:

Exactly!

Matthew:

That is so good. I am so happy that you are leading me. I am so happy to know this.

God:

I am a good God — wise and all knowing. Sometimes, you learn so much from deception. Your teaching and sharing is so much more powerful with so much more authority when you have come through deception. When you have been deceived and come to the other side to know the truth, then you can reach back and help others out of that same deception.

For this reason, when you find people on Facebook in deception, you should not argue with them but simply love them and pray for them to come out of it. I am a wise God. I know what I am doing in the lives of my people. You don't have to always be right; it is ok to leave a person in their deception and pray for them.

Matthew:

I know a person that you're talking about here. I will do that. I will focus on loving him rather than trying to correct him now.

God:

Ok. I hope you were blessed by this conversation. I hope you are more comfortable. Be at peace.

Chapter 7
Fresh Ideas

God:

Hello, Matthew. How are you today?

Matthew:

I am a bit tired. I have had trouble with my mind being foggy.

God:

Well, today's topic should wake you up. I want to talk to you about how we lead you. We like to be your source and inspire you so that everything that you do has our hand in it. We like it when you co-labor with us.

Matthew:

Does it happen often?

God:

Yes, in your life, it happens more than you know. We led you to the picture on this book. We lead you with what you say in this book. We lead you each day. A combination of the Holy Spirt, Jesus, I and your angels lead you. Each day, we give you direction and thoughts to lead you to do certain things. You are so pliable to us. Many times, you think you had your own idea, but we planted the idea in your mind.

Matthew:

How can people get to that stage?

God:

Well, you started to walk in the Spirit and be led by us when you started to actively obey the commands of Jesus in your life. We used those commands as a framework so that you got used to following the Holy Spirit in obedience. As you learned to rely on him each day, it became really natural to you.

Now you obey my Spirit without consciously knowing it. You are so sensitive to him that we find it very easy to direct you. People can open up their minds and ask us what they need to do in each situation. We will direct them in the way that we want them to decide. It really comes down to their choice. A person needs to let go and simply give their life and their decisions over to us. When they are directed by us, then they truly have built their lives on the rock.

Matthew:

Some people don't want to let go of control.

God:

People don't want to let go of control for a number of reasons. They fear that if they let go of control, circumstances won't work out for them. It's as scary to them as taking their hands off the steering wheel of a car that they are driving. They fear if they let go, their lives will crash. They don't let go because they instinctively fear that I don't have their best interests in mind due to their misunderstanding of me and my ways. Many people think that I want to destroy the fun in their life.

Many people think that my plan for their life is not as exciting as their own plans. But the truth is that my ideas and plans for a person's life are why they were created. Many people think that they know themselves and know what they want best, yet I know people better than they know themselves. I have the perfect plans for their life. By giving me control of their lives, they actually live the life that they were created to live. I don't move against a person's will, but I will direct a person to places and decisions that they would not have made for themselves.

Matthew:

Tell me more.

God:

You see, Matthew, we have a perfect plan for your life. We know the books you will write. We know the best covers for those books. We know the content that will be useful with each of those books. We lead you to read certain books to give you the information you need to write books in the future. Each of our decisions in your life prepare you for your future books. Each time we inspire people to give to your ministry account, we have a use for that money, and we lead you on how to spend it. We lead you step by step and decision by decision so that you can do a much better job than if you made your own decisions.

We draw so close to you and become such a part of your life that each of your ideas and thoughts comes from us. We direct you in all that you do so that you do what we want you to do. When you walk with us, your life becomes so given over to us that we can do miraculous things with you.

Matthew:

I guess that is because I trust you. If a person doesn't trust you, then they would struggle to follow your lead and your ideas.

God:

Yes, a person needs to come to a place where they trust us. They need to know that we have their best life prepared for them if they let go of the steering wheel by faith. They need to follow us by faith and not walk by sight. The sad thing is that most people in the world want to walk by sight. Most people want to know what is ahead. They have trouble trusting us for each step, and they are used to planning their own steps, so they find it hard to relinquish control to us.

For example, you don't know what your next book will be about yet, Matthew, but you are not worried about it. You simply work on the book that you are doing and wait for us to inspire you for the next one. People need to trust that our ideas and our direction is best for them. When the time comes for a fresh direction in their life, they can depend on us to give them a fresh idea.

Matthew:

I guess I know that now. I am used to being directed by you guys. But I imagine that it can be a scary subject for some people, especially for those people with trust issues.

God:

Yes, people need to get to know us. When you learn to obey Jesus in all he taught, you find out that his ways are best. When you do what he taught, you learn that he can be trusted. Then you can learn to trust us to direct you in all parts of your life.

You need to come to the understanding that we are right and that our directions are best for you. The key to knowing Jesus and therefore me is found in obeying Jesus' commands.

Matthew:

I know; I did this. I didn't realize that I would come to trust Jesus. I guess so much wisdom lies in that. I was wondering how you were going to show people how to come to a place where they can trust you. I thought you were going to quote a book that I have read so they could trust you guys.

God:

The gospel is simple. Anything that makes the gospel hard is not the true gospel. People need to know what Jesus taught and take the step and start to obey it. Through obeying Jesus, they will come to know him, and he will manifest what he is like to them. "He who has My commandments and keeps them, it is he who loves Me. And he who loves Me will be loved by My Father, and I will love him and manifest Myself to him" (John 14: 21).

Matthew:

You are amazing. You speak so simply. I have been amazed that you have not been speaking with really profound speech but in a simple manner through these conversations. I am glad because many more people will understand. I am so happy that you are sharing your thoughts and ideas with us. I am so glad that you have been leading me. It is my prayer that everyone who reads this will come to know you as a God that cares and loves them and who wants to lead them.

God:

Be blessed, Matthew.

Chapter 8
Rest in My Love

God:

Hello, Matthew, how are you today?

Matthew:

I am awake. I am looking forward to what you have to say today. I am enjoying our conversations. I am being touched by you.

God:

I have so much in me and so much that I want you to know. Do you know that I love people with a love that is hot like a fire? I have an unquenchable love for my people. I love the whole world, but those that have accepted Jesus into their lives hold a special place in my heart. I have so many things that I want to show my people. A large part of the Christian journey is for individuals to come to an understanding that I love them and for them to rest in my love. When a person thinks that they have to do something to earn my love, they are never at rest and are continually trying to prove their love to me.

Matthew:

I was like that for many years. I thought that I had to do all these things to be accepted by you. I thought that holiness was a mode of behavior and not a position in which I could rest.

God:

Many people have a list of rules and obligations that they feel they have to meet before they are holy in my sight, so they spend their whole lives trying to maintain their place with me. They don't consider or have never been taught that Jesus met every requirement that I needed, so all they need to do is find me and rest in my love.

Matthew:

It is hard, God. We think we need to do something to please you. We can even follow the commandments of Jesus religiously as a means to earn your love. Even Jesus' commands were part of my religious duty at one time. It goes against our flesh to believe that we have been accepted by you just as we are. Part of us thinks that we always have to earn your love. Few of us know that we are loved as much as Jesus and that we are fully accepted and beloved. This is a struggle, and while we struggle, we are not resting in your love.

God:

It is a struggle for many people. Man thinks he has to earn my love, so he goes to all these lengths to prove my love. Instead, he simply needs to relax in my grace and let my love and power clean him up. It is simple, but the religious teaching and mindsets in people refuse to let them believe what is clear as day. If the sacrifice of my Son was not enough to clean up people, what more could I possibly do? Satan really has the church bound in false teaching. Good, honest pastors and priests all over the world are teaching a gospel that says you need the sacrifice of Jesus plus good works to inherit the Kingdom of God. Instead, when you accept that Christ is enough and rest in him, then good works will naturally follow. The commandments of Jesus are important to follow to find me and to learn how to walk in the Spirit, but they need to be approached from a state of rest.

Matthew:

In the past few years, I have begun to rest in your love. As a result, I have been striving less and less.

God:

Yes, you are in a good place now, Matthew. But you used to strive to please me. For many years, you lived an external life and didn't possess the Kingdom internally. Now, you have become a little child, and you walk in a simple faith. You are very much led by our Holy Spirit. These days, you minister from a place of rest. Now you are comfortable. But it was not always that way for you.

Matthew:

I wasn't sure that you were happy with me. I thought I had to do something to earn your love. The problem with having to earn love is that you can never be sure that you have done enough. I was in this cycle of writing articles and giving free prophecies to make you happy. No matter how much I performed, I felt that I always fell short.

God:

That is why people have to understand the gospel of grace. Until they know that Christ's death was enough for them, they will wander around the wilderness all of their Christian lives and never enter the land of promise into my rest. When you live in that place of love and acceptance from me, and you minister from a place of rest, your ministry can become so powerful. Instead of just using the anointing to achieve things in ministry, you have this strong endurance as part of your makeup, allowing you to take time out to seek me at any time. People that don't have a place of rest don't ever take time out to be refreshed, and they find their sense of self-esteem through doing ministry. This place of always "doing" ministry to feel worthwhile inevitability leads to burnout.

Matthew:

I have been there, God. I have been burned out in the prophetic two times. And yes, you are right. That happened when I looked to find my esteem from ministry. Now, my esteem is to be in a right place with you. Now when I don't feel like doing anything for the Kingdom, I take the day off. I don't beat myself up about it but simply take a break. I never used to be able to do that. I told my mother that I didn't write a chapter of this book yesterday, and I took a day off. She reminded me that years ago, when I was bound by religion, I wouldn't have been able to do that.

God:

People need to be free of guilt and condemnation. They have to be free to be themselves. They have to be free not to have to always perform. Like you, they need to be able to have a day off and watch TV or sleep. People need to be taught that they are perfect right now. They have to understand that I love them exactly how they are. They have to stop thinking that they must overcome a particular sin or habit before I will accept them. They have to know that I love and understand them now. They have to know that they will only overcome the sin in their lives when they rest in my love and grace. Whenever they strive to overcome sin, their consciousness of that sin will lead them to sin even more. People who don't understand this concept should buy the book "Destined to Reign" by Joseph Prince.

Matthew:

That book taught me so much, but I seem to have misplaced it now. It is really funny to see you as God recommending a book.

God:

Why does it seem funny? I use books to train people since they are great resources for people to learn about all kinds of subjects. I will recommend your books to people and move people by the Holy Spirit to buy them. One of the reasons that you are a writer is to better educate people. Of course I will mention a book. If people are feeling condemned and don't understand how religion works against you, they need to read books to help them. I also think your book, "Your Identity in Christ," would help these readers know how we see them.

Matthew:

It is so good talking to you. I am so pleased that you are not talking in profound language that is hard to understand. I am pleased you are speaking in words and sentences that are easy to understand. You are good to us.

God:

I have a lot in my heart to share with the people of this world. I want them to know that I love them and that they are forgiven. I even want people who don't know Jesus to know that I made a way for them through his death. I want all people to know that I love them and have a purpose for their lives. I think it is best to speak plainly so that more people will understand. I speak to the mystics in deep and profound language, but I speak to you plainly so that more people can read and comprehend what I am saying. I want to be a God that is near and welcoming and loving. I don't want people to need 30 years as a Christian to understand what I am saying. I want all of the readers to understand me.

Matthew:

Thank you for speaking to me today.

God:

It was my pleasure, Matthew.

Chapter 9
Fresh Manna

God:

How are you today, Matthew?

Matthew:

I have been stuck. I had a pause in our conversations. I have missed you. Today, I slept a lot.

God:

It's ok, Matthew. Everyone has good and bad days. I noticed last night at church that you were sad. It's ok to be sad or down. Sometimes, your depression is too much for you. I understand that.

Matthew:

I am looking forward to hearing you speak to me. I am really enjoying our conversations. I decided to sit down and listen to what you had to say because I missed you.

God:

That is how I want everyone to feel. I want them to come to me each day whether or not they are going through a bit of depression. I want to be the bread of life to each person. I want people to become so used to me that they cannot do without me. That is why these conversations are so good for you. They give you a taste of who I am each day. When you go two days without me, I want you to return to me with a sense of expectancy. I want to be your daily bread, your fresh manna.

Matthew:

It is comforting to talk to you. You understand me. You understand all of us, including the readers. You know everything about us. To put it simply, you know how we feel. You know all about our lives; you know our weaknesses. You know what we need to hear. You know what to say to lift our spirits. I have been in a funk, a dip of depression, and it is a little sad.

God:

Yes, I know. I am not a God without feelings. I can come inside you and feel how you are feeling. I can feel your emotions — your sadness. And I know that your sadness doesn't come from anywhere except the fact that it is an attack on your life. That is why I want to be your daily portion. Part of you wants to retreat and pull away from people when you are depressed. Part of you wants to withdraw, even from us in heaven who care for you. It is a sad thing, but we want to be your source. We want to be the ones that you run to. Whenever any person is suffering, we want to be their solace and the source that they run to. We want to be familiar with you. We want to lead and comfort you. We want to be your everything.

Matthew:

Why do we run **from** you when we suffer? Why don't we run **to** you?

God:

It's part of the enemy's plan to shut you down. The enemy tries to make you believe that no one can understand you and that no one wants to help you. You withdraw because it takes feelings to talk to someone, and when you're hurting, your feelings are tender and raw. You do the opposite of what you should do. You think that you don't want to burden anyone with your sad thoughts, yet people that love you can help you with those very thoughts. You should know that nothing is too much of a burden for us who love you. Jesus and I love every part of you. We love you in the good times and in the sad times. Do you know that satan tried to shut you down this time because you are doing a good job with these conversations?

Matthew:

It makes sense. He tries to shut down every good thing that I do. It is such a struggle sometimes.

God:

That is why we love for you to come to us each day to be refreshed. Jesus came to me every day when he was on earth. He suffered, too; he had bad thoughts and hurt feelings. He suffered more than many people realize. His life was a struggle also. Every day, satan was against him, trying to make him sin. You are not the first person to struggle, Matthew. We have been with people through the centuries since Christ, and we will be with you every step of the way through your life.

I have so much love and respect for you. You have no idea how much I really love you. I love you so much. If you could grasp my great love for you, you would not worry so much. I have so much to teach you through these experiences. You can gain so much knowledge and wisdom as you go through your life. Each day and each week, we have new things to show you. We want you to know that we have you covered.

Matthew:

That is so comforting to hear. Sometimes, when my depression comes on me, I feel hopeless. I feel that I am not going to be able to cope. I need to know that you are going to see me through and that you have my back.

God:

We are here for you and for everybody. Some people might look at your life, Matthew, and be jealous of your relationship with us and your ability to hear from us, yet it would help them to know that you have your struggles and hard times also. You live in a world that is hard on many people. The world has a lot of suffering. People need to know us and come to us and let us speak to them and help them find a way through life.

Just like the Israelites collected manna each day in the wilderness to survive, people should make a practice of coming to us each day for their daily bread. We don't say that life on earth is simple. Jesus shared that in your life, you are going to have tribulations. He wanted to bring you comfort because he overcame the world. You, too, can overcome the world and its devices by clinging to us and resting in us. It is interesting that after you wrote about the subject of rest, you were attacked so badly. It seems that resting in us really is the answer. I am the One that loves you all. I am your Creator and your God. Come rest in me.

Matthew:

I am feeling better now that I have been talking to you. Your words are bringing me comfort. You know how to speak right to my heart. It makes a lot of sense because you know how I am feeling. You told me that you can feel what I am feeling. I must learn to come to you each time depression overcomes me rather than running from everyone.

God:

You will learn in time. You will grasp it. It takes practice and time spent together to grow in trust. A person cannot decide to get close to me and accomplish this after a prayer in just one day. Like any relationship, it takes hours and hours of conversation to grow close and develop trust and vulnerability with each other. People should not expect to have an awesome relationship with me overnight.

A relationship with me can be found by watching a DVD or YouTube video or reading a book. Those things point a person to me. A person that has a great relationship with me can write a book about how to draw near to me, but the reader still needs to apply the teaching through many hours of their time and patience. I need to be part of their daily lives to be of any lasting effect.

Matthew:

You are so wise, God. I know I should not be surprised. You say such simple things, but they have so much depth and wisdom to them. This book is really helping me get to know you. I am happy that I sat down today to type this chapter.

God:

You had an angel that helped you sit down and get in the mood. Even when you sat down, you did not want to write. Yet as I spoke to you, you started to feel the change in yourself so that now, you are feeling good. The same goes for other people. You won't always be in the mood to come to me. You won't always want to set time aside and speak to me or read your Bible. But when you do, as my Spirit comes upon you, you, too, will find joy and peace rise up within you as you fellowship with me. I have a way with my creation.

You see, this happen many times in the Psalms. David starts out crying to me to help him, and at the conclusion of the Psalm, he is thanking me for coming to his rescue. I want to meet with my people. I want to be your daily manna. Be blessed, Matthew.

Chapter 10
Be Content

God:

Hello, Matthew. How are you?

Matthew:

I was just in bed, thinking of going to sleep when your Holy Spirit told me to get up and write this chapter. It is a funny thing. Many times, I do my best work in the middle of the night when most of the world is sleeping. You are funny.

God:

I am glad that you find me funny. Yes, it is great to catch you when you are wide awake, and you really do operate well in the middle of the night. You weren't sure that you were tired enough to go to sleep, and here we have you up, writing the next chapter. The good thing about you, Matthew, is that you are so pliable to us. You nearly always do what we want you to do. We rarely ask you to do something that you don't do. Do you know how happy that makes us feel? We are so excited to have you in our lives. You are a joy to us. I sometimes wish that every believer not only heard from us as clearly as you do, but that they would also be as obedient to us as you are. You were quite within your rights to try and go to sleep or to watch a video and ignore us, but here you are, doing what we wanted you to do.

Matthew:

It's a good subject, Lord. I am pretty content with my life. Today, I sent off my manuscript to my editor for my second book on angels. I am feeling really good about that. Then, I started to do the last read through to "A Beginner's Guide to the Prophetic" before I am due to send that off to the editor at the end of the month when my book royalties come in that will cover the cost of editing. I live a life of contentment. I don't worry about too much. I am pretty simple to please.

God:

Yes, you are easy to please. You are happy whenever you have a project to do, and you are busy. You like to stay busy, and we keep you busy. We have TV shows on DVD that you watch to relax and kick back. When we have a TV series for you to watch, we see you enjoy yourself. You read a book from time to time and learn from them and find things to share in your books. You are pretty simple to please. You don't have many needs. You don't have the amount of lusts that the average person has.

You are always content, which is one of the keys to a life that is filled with joy and prosperity. You're a person with simple desires who is patient about their future and what has been promised through prophecy, and it is really easy to please you. Even though all your books are not bestsellers, you get excited each time someone buys and reads one. You are an easy person to please.

Matthew:

I don't know what made me so simple. I don't know why I don't lust for things that other people lust after. I simply have no desire for money, possessions or a good name among men. I live to please you and do what I was created to do. Writing brings me joy, and I will happily write books until the time comes when you open doors for me to preach from church to church. Each month, hundreds of people download my books, and I feel that I am going all around the world and ministering to people in their homes with my books. I am so happy and so fulfilled.

I have few needs and few desires, and while I am not married, I can quite happily spend my money on furthering your kingdom. I delight to write. I love to have people write to me. I love to prophesy. I love reading reviews on my books. I love my life. It really doesn't take much to please me. I wish that I could teach other people how to be so content with their lives rather than hoping for a better life and more fulfilment. You have to stop wishing for a better future and learn to be content with where you are and what you have at the moment. Contentment is my secret.

God:

You have such a wonderful heart. You have the heart of a spiritual father. You have a heart that wants to encourage people and teach them. You would give your whole life to educating others and encouraging them how to live in the Spirit and how to live a life that sees them doing what they were created to do. Your whole heart is focused on pleasing me and helping others. You have no desires of your own that do not include blessing me or blessing others. That is so rare. I wish that all people could capture your heart on these matters.

I wish that everyone could find their purpose and live it out. I wish that you could train people to be like yourself. I know that you are going to write books in the future that teach people these things, but sometimes, I wish I could have you teach the entire body of Christ how to live a Christian life. We are going to promote you and take you to the world because people need to know how to live a life full of purpose, destiny and contentment. They need to know how to love me and do my will and stop their love affair with the world and all that it offers.

Matthew:

My heart aches for you, Father. I love the people of God, but it is so hard to talk to people about the things that matter. That is why I like communicating through books. At least a person searches for the type of the book that they want. They find a book and read the back cover and read a few reviews on Amazon, and then, they download it if they like what they read. Then, once a person has my book, I have a hundred or more pages to make my argument.

People will not be bored in print. So if one of my books doesn't capture them, and they become bored with it, they put it down. But if they are excited by it, they will read the whole book and, hopefully, make the changes that I suggest. I am so excited that people are buying my books and choosing to read them. I sometimes wish that I could meet the people that read my books. I am excited when they friend me on Facebook and chat with me and tell me what they liked about my books. You really have given me an exciting life, Father.

God:

I have had this life of yours planned before my Son went to the cross. I have waited for you to come for centuries. I have raised you up and given you my knowledge and my wisdom and and kept you as my secret treasure. You are my secret weapon. You are going to see things that not many people see. You are growing so close to me, and you are so obedient that I am going to direct kings and leaders of countries through your counsel. I am going to use you to do mighty works. You are going to change the world like Moses changed his world when he lived. You were born for such a time as this.

You are not a mistake, and the enemy has attacked you so viciously because you have a big and long-lasting future. You're going to rock your country; you are going to rock the world, and many lives are going to be affected by you. You don't seem to grasp where I have you headed. But you are not a mistake. You are still hidden now, but in years to come, the whole world will know who you are. You are so simple. You are so easy to please. You are so patient, and you're such a dear friend to us that we are going to look after you and use you as our last days' weapon.

Matthew:

It fills me with such joy to hear you speak about me like this. It's like you're giving me a prophecy over my life. I have heard most of this in other prophecies, but it makes me so happy to have you repeat it. It means so much to me for you to say that I wasn't a mistake. My father told me that I was the result of an unplanned pregnancy. My father told me a few times that I was a mistake. I am so refreshed to hear that you planned me before Christ died. I want to be that weapon in your arsenal. I look forward to the day that I am speaking to hundreds of people. I look forward to having a book table and a staff and then having people buy the books that I have written that will equip them. You make me so happy. My life is so good. Even though satan attacks me with depression, and I am lonely at times, I am happy to be known and loved by you guys.

God:

The proper Christian life is such a simple process to talk about but so hard for people to walk out. People need to know us; people need to speak to us and learn to hear from us. People need to know their purpose and then do what they were created to do. People need to flee the world and its lusts and to choose us over the world.

These seem like simple steps, but many Christians don't ever achieve them during their whole lives. I know your life purpose is to teach people these things. You, like us, want the people of God to rise up and become all that they were created to be. It is a burden on your heart. You cannot get rid of it.

It is a common theme in all of your books. It does not matter how many times you share it; it does not matter how many people hear you; it does not matter how many millions of people you teach this to; the fact remains that everyone has free will and can choose to apply or reject it. And that is what makes you sad and what breaks my heart. People don't want to leave the world; they don't want to follow me, and they don't want to change to do what they were destined to do. It is so sad. If people don't learn to be content in this life, they will always be chasing after the things of the world and will never reach the place that you are, my son, Matthew.

Matthew:

This is sad. I hope people pay attention to this chapter. I am sure that people that read this would not want to make you sad. It has broken my heart to hear you say this. I feel your heart. I will have to listen to some worship and praise you a little to restore my happiness. I went from being full of joy to really sad. This chapter has been a real roller coaster. I suppose that is why I am a prophet. I guess you will not always give me a happy message for others.

God:

Thanks for listening, Matthew. I don't always have happy messages for you to pass on. Be blessed.

Chapter 11
The Fire

God:

Welcome, Matthew. It's good to be with you.

Matthew:

I have been suffering from depression and have had issues with my sleep, and I have not been coming to you each day. I have missed you and missed our time together, but while I had this heavy feeling, I couldn't bring myself to write.

God:

I understand, Matthew. We love you. We are upset when you are upset. But today, you are back, and today, you have the energy to sit down and hear from us. I love speaking to you and the readers of this book. Some people don't understand that we care about everything. In heaven, nothing is ignored or swept under the carpet. We are aware of everything, and we care. I watch you and see the struggle that you go through and wish that you could be whole and not suffer.

Matthew:

It makes me glad that you care. I guess people seem to think that you don't have the time to care about every little detail in their lives. We are fooled into thinking other people are more deserving of your time and your energy. Sometimes, we think that the people that are more popular in your kingdom receive the majority of your attention. It is comforting to know that you care for me. It's amazing how the enemy works in our lives and convinces us that you don't care.

God:

I am your Creator, Matthew. I know you better then anyone. I know you better then your angels, better then your sisters in heaven and better then your parents. I made you. I have a lot to do with what you think and what you care about.

I have placed my fire in your life. I have given you a fire that burns within your heart. I have given you a reason to live and a reason to speak. I have given you your message that burns bright in your heart. You are consumed by it like a living, burning bush. You are consumed by my fire, but you are not extinguished. I have called you to live and breathe my message to the world.

Matthew:

It's funny that you call me a burning bush because that is how I feel. I am consumed by the fire within my heart, but I am not burned up. I am excited and intense and passionate all at once. So much has to be done in this world. People need to understand so much, including all that they have to do. Sometimes, I am surprised that people don't know what I know. I wonder if it is because they lack the ability to find out the answers or if they are happy with the world and its fleshy ways and they simply don't care?

God:

It is both, Matthew. As a teacher, you are different to many people. You come to life with questions and an inquiring mind. You are not comfortable with the status quo and what is accepted, and you are always on a journey to know more and teach more. Secondly, you have come out of the world with all its lusts, and you have a vested interest in what is right, and you have my heart for people, so you really care.

If people are not teachers, they can't be expected to search out things like you do, but people can be taught how to come out of the world and how to serve me rather then the lusts of the flesh. They can learn what it looks to deny oneself, take up their cross and follow in the footsteps of my Son, Jesus. You know that you have to teach people how to do this. You know you have to encourage people to live a life that is set apart for me and my glory. You have so much to teach people. And that fire endlessly rages in your heart.

Matthew:

It is hard for me to imagine people not knowing what I know because I assume they know these things. Then, I look around and find that I am unique, and I have a lonely path. It is hard to consider what is wrong with the world, what the church can do about it and how each individual can change. It makes me cry sometimes. So many people need to be loved, appreciated and shown the light, yet the average Christian doesn't even know how to do that. So few Christians seem to know how to be the light in their world. Sometimes it makes me so sad to contemplate.

God:

Welcome to our world. Two thousand years ago, my Son, Jesus, shared with the world how to be light. Now the people of God have learned how to be religious, to run churches, do worship, pay tithes and fill churches with people, yet not many of them know how to imitate Jesus in their world. Jesus came as a model; the disciples recorded a lot of what he taught, so what is so hard about people doing what he taught? People are so caught up with their personal lives, earning a living and being entertained in their downtime that they do not know how to live the optimal Christian life that the first believers lived. You feel the fire in your heart, Matthew, and the desire to teach my people. You have a burning desire to lead my people out of the bondage of their Egypt to the Promised Land, yet the people in bondage don't even know that they are in bondage.

Matthew:

So much has to be taught to others. Sometimes, I wonder why you need to use me. Surely, enough teachers and prophets can accomplish this work. Why did you choose me to have this fire in my heart? Why do I have to suffer this burning and these tears for your people? Surely, there are enough prophets in the world. Why can't I just forget what I know and go back to being an ordinary Christian with no worries or concerns about the church?

God:

Because we have fashioned you for this. We created you to listen to our frequency. We made you to be like you are, and we molded your heart to be soft and pliable. We put a heart in you like that of Moses, and we raised you up to be a prophet. You think like us. You feel like us. I need many people like you, ordinary folk to find you and relate to you. You alone will reach certain people, and the big name ministries won't have as much of an effect on them. I need you, Matthew.

I need everyone that is willing to help me. I want the world to change. I want the church to know me like you know me. I don't want to speak through pastors, teachers and prophets; I want to speak to people face to face. I want the church to know me and have my heart for the nations, which is why I need to use you to teach a group of people what I want them to hear. I need you to teach people how to come to me. While I need you, the fire will burn in your heart.

Have a good day, Matthew.

Chapter 12
Alone

God:

Hi, Matthew, how are you today?

Matthew:

I am good. I have had enough sleep. Depression does not seem to be around today. I am looking forward to speaking with you. This is a subject that I relate to very much.

God:

Yes, I do a great work in many of my people, and they seem to find themselves alone in this world. It is like they lose touch with the world that they live in. This is not by design or choice, but they seem to pull away from the world and all its lusts. You are one that travels alone in this world, and we are proud of you for this.

Matthew:

It makes for a lonely life. I have to say that it hurts to be alone in this world. It is not a great feeling. I long to know more people and have substantial relationships, but it seems that the people that I know don't seem to be passionate about you and your kingdom. I can't settle for any less than everything that you have to offer. I cannot compromise my beliefs and my passion for you and all that you have for me.

God:

We made you this way, Matthew. We led you to this place. We have separated you from the crowd. We have taken you from the mass of Christians, and we have led you into a lonely place that is set apart and separate. You have been chosen by us to be alone yet in your relationship with us to be a powerful influence on others.

Every time you speak in your Facebook groups and every time you interact with people, you share with authority. You are one that has spent time with us and people recognize that fact. You speak with the authority of one who has spent time with the living God.

Matthew:

I am glad that you said that about me. Sometimes, I think my words aren't even making a difference. I am sometimes disheartened that people are not listening and learning in my groups that I run. It is sometimes hard for me to realize that I have a different relationship with you than most other people. It is hard to comprehend that others do not know you like I do. I wish that they all knew you the way that I do. Even with all that I know about Jesus, I wish that I knew you better.

God:

If you know Jesus, you know me. If you have seen Jesus, you have seen me. I am the One who sustains you. I am your source. I am the One that has drawn you to myself and taught you. Though you have been talking to Jesus all your life, you have also been talking to me. You don't have to spend more time getting to know me. For Jesus is the way to me. I am the truth that you have sought out and that you know.

I am your Redeemer and your Friend. Together, we are going to change the world that you live in and make a difference. You are going to be a powerful force and voice to this generation, and this is only the start of it. These books are only the beginning. Through these books, you have the ability to hear me speak, but soon, I will be with you every day in the same way that you have known Jesus in your past. I am going to work through you and use you to do great things.

Matthew:

It is so good to hear you speak to me, and I am so excited. Being alone is so much easier when I have the Trinity as friends. I also have the saints and angels to keep me company. I like that every one of them, including you guys, knows me intimately and even better then myself. It is so good hanging out with others that know me so well. I don't have to prove myself to you guys. You know every part of me — my past, my future and what I have to do each day to get to my future. You all lead me and know me, and you all have a part to play in my life. I may lack people on earth to mix with and interact with, but I have many of you from heaven to keep me company.

God:

Yes, we are here for you. We want you to be like you are. We have designed you to be alone. We know it is hard, but we know if you had plenty of friends, you would need us less. And we need some people on earth that are totally committed to us. We need some people on earth that have uncompromised faith. We need people that we can use as an untainted voice to bring messages to the world. Any person that finds themselves alone can use that opportunity to draw close to us.

We are ready to draw close to any person, especially those who find themselves alone. We won't reject them, and we will use them. We will complete their lives just as we complete yours. You see, we could allow you to have many friends, but in order for that to happen, you would have to lose some of the fire that is within you. We have many followers that lack fire. We don't need any more people that are cold and lukewarm. We need living stones that are on fire.

Matthew:

I understand. I am sure that it is because of my loneliness that I reach out to so many people though prophetic evangelism. I like to simply interact with people, so I use every opportunity to speak to people. I think it is because I am alone that I write so much. My need to speak has me writing, which comforts me. I know some of my readers are blessed, and it really does my heart good to get burdens off my chest. So I know that a few things happen because I am alone. I know that I would not be nearly as close to you guys if I had plenty of friends. Being alone has so many benefits. Even with all those benefits, it is still hard for me.

God:

Yes, Matthew, we know that this and many things in your life are hard on you. But like a fine wine brought from crushed grapes, we know that the crushing of you brings out the sweetest essence of you. It is through your testing and refining that we are able to shine through you. It is through you being alone that we have the opportunity to work through you so powerfully. Everything is as it should be. It is our grand design. And our way is the best way for you.

It is nothing that you have done. You are not alone because you are a jerk or because you are not loving. You are alone because of our design, and we are the ones who are glorified through your life. We are the ones who are happy with who you are and all that you do. You are ours and that makes us very happy and contented.

Matthew:

It is my pleasure to please you in all that I say and do. I wonder how much the readers will learn from it. It seems that this isn't about them but all about you and your purpose in my life. I wonder if this is boring for them. But I guess that those people that love you and are passionate about you have a similar life. You have similar lessons in this for those who want to be close to you. Those that are lonely will also find answers. The enemy is trying to make me worry and to stop writing, and I am not going to stop because I am enjoying speaking to you.

God:

That is right. This book isn't for everyone. To some, it might be irrelevant and boring. We are not after them but are after the ones that are hot for us, the ones that have a fire in their hearts. We are after the ones that want to walk hand in hand with us. This book will be a guide, a comfort and a great resource to those people that have a great relationship with us.

This book will encourage many to start their own journals with us and will open their eyes to what is possible. Yes, the enemy wants you to stop. He does not like this and does not want to see it come into print. That is his problem. He doesn't like any of your books. You have to just press on and do what you are destined to do with your life and my words.

Matthew:

I really like hearing you explain things. You really have a simple way of teaching me. Yes, we are after the hot ones, the burning ones, the ones that are on fire. You make so much sense to me.

God:

You are a delight to me, warm and engaging. You are patient and obedient. This book wouldn't be written without you sitting down and giving us your time and your energy. You are vital to this message. We delight in everything that you do. You may live a lonely life for the company of earthly humans, but you don't live a lonely life for visitors from heaven.

Many people read your books and wish that they had your relationship with us. Well, your relationship comes at great personal cost. Your relationship with us didn't come from one prayer or one impartation; it came from many years of suffering and prayer. It is still maintained through much tribulation. You are kept hot and on fire by our design. Your faith and walk with us is not easy to achieve. It is not cheap. It can't be found in one book. People have to apply what you teach them. But the good thing about your life and your testimony is that your life and intimacy with us is possible for others also. This chapter has gone on long enough now. I'll bid you goodbye.

Matthew:

Bye.

Chapter 13
Imitate Jesus

God:

Hi, Matthew. This is the second message from me that you are doing today. You are in a good mood and are ready to type.

Matthew:

Yes. I am in a good mood and was open to doing another message. To be honest, I wasn't finished speaking to you about the last message of being alone. I was enjoying myself so much that I wanted to continue, so here we are.

God:

This lesson is all about how I want people to imitate Jesus in the world. I need the world to be blessed with lives that are full of love and mercy. I need people to be giving, compassionate and caring to others. I need people to touch the lives of others. I need my people who honor my Son to live and act like him. I am looking for lovers. I am looking for people to spread love all around the world where they live. I need people to make a difference to the world.

You just finished reading the book, "Following the Rabbi," by Daniel Skillman, and it really touched you. It was a book about the message of Jesus and what people on earth are called to do if they are Christians. I planned for you to read that book, and I am so impressed that it touched you so deeply. People really need to know what Jesus was like, and they really need to start to live like he did. John wrote this in the scriptures about the Christian life. "He who says he abides in Him ought himself also to walk just as

He walked" (1 John 2:6). John says that a person that says that they are walking hand in hand with Jesus should walk and act like Jesus did. Many people live lives that are quite far from this standard and excuse themselves by saying that they are just sinners.

Matthew:

Yes, that verse is convicting but also very encouraging. John lived a life like that, or he could not have written that verse. He knew that it was not only possible to walk like Jesus, but he had been doing it personally. I know that Paul said twice in scripture, "Imitate me, just as I also imitate Christ" (1 Corinthians 11:1, 4:16). Paul would not tell people to imitate him as he imitates Christ if he wasn't already doing it.

God:

That is so true, Matthew. The big lie out there is that Paul was a sinner who could not control his sin life. People think that if Paul wrote about his struggle with sin, then they, too, are excused from living a holy life. But people do not know that Paul conquered his sin life and lived in a new creation reality. They do not know that Paul taught that you can live a holy and set-apart life. People assume that sin will always be with them and that they can't overcome it, so they should not even try.

Paul wrote, "But now having been set free from sin, and having become slaves of God, you have your fruit to holiness, and the end, everlasting life" (Romans 6:22). You can be set free from sin; you can live free of it, and you can walk on this earth just like Jesus did. Paul taught this by telling people to imitate him. Peter taught that you can be holy. John taught that you can live without sin. The Christian life holds a lot more than most people know. You can be transformed and live just like my Son.

Matthew:

It is amazing. It is so refreshing to know.

God:

The people of God need to know what is possible. They need to know that they are gods, and they can be divine, perfected and refined to live holy and precious lives. They need to know that they can be fruit-bearing trees of righteousness.

He shall be like a tree

Planted by the rivers of water,

That brings forth its fruit in season,

Whose leaf also shall not wither;

And whatever he does shall prosper (Psalm 1:3).

Matthew:

That is one of my favorite verses in the Bible.

God:

Yes, you can be a tree that bears fruit for the sustenance of others, for people to come and eat. You can go through hard times of spiritual drought, and your leaves will not wither. You can live a life in which everything that you do prospers. You can live this verse. When you are living this verse, your life has become like that of my Son's. I have so much more for people and can do so much for them.

People have so much capacity in them. They just need to know what is possible — to not only be a source of freedom for others and a source of comfort for people but to live a life of abundance so that they have enough to be a supply for the needs of others. People only live substandard lives because they are not aware of what the Holy Spirit can do through them.

Matthew:

Many of the things I do now are prospering. I have become a source of overflowing supply for people. I have become a fruitful tree. I have begun to prosper and been sovereignly supplied by you. I can testify to this happening in my life.

God:

Yes, we are doing that in your life so that you can testify about it. When we do great things in your life, you can share them with others. You can say, "Hey guys, all this is possible." You can share that following us can be of great benefit to them. Jesus lived with everything that he needed each day. He not only had the anointing and power to heal every sickness, but he had a monetary supply so that he could do everything that we wanted him to do.

He had boundless compassion and love, and he transformed every person that we wanted transformed. He was very powerful, which caused the world to kill him. He was obedient, even to a gruesome death on a cross.

Matthew:

Yes, he gave his whole life. He lived every day to do your will. The good news is that we can also do that. We can also be used powerfully.

God:

That is right. You can live a life that affects many people. You can change the world and the people in it through your witness and your faith. Every single person has a number of people that they can influence. They can bring healing, happiness and joy to others where they live. They can be flames of love and can light up the world. They don't have to change everyone in the whole world; they just need to affect the people that they know and that they do life with. Any person, no matter how popular they are, can affect people. Every person that leans into us and who draws close to us can have a lasting affect on other people. Anyone that has my Spirit can live like Jesus and change people.

Matthew:

That is so encouraging. You are so encouraging. It is important for us to know that we don't have to change the whole world; we simply need to have a good and loving affect on the people that we know. We don't have to be the most popular person in the world, but we can be a powerful force on the people that you choose us to influence.

God:

This is true, Matthew. You will never be able to speak to the whole world. No matter how important you become, no matter how powerful you become, you will never reach everyone. Therefore, what is important is for you to be effective among the people with whom you have an audience. Jesus was the most anointed man to live on the earth. He could heal every sickness, and he possessed all knowledge of the Kingdom. However, not even Jesus had an impact on everyone when he was here. Everyone in the world still does not know of him even with modern media. Therefore, you will never reach the whole world, but you are called to live and move in the Spirit at every opportunity so that your words and actions aren't wasted among the people that we call you to reach. We want you to have a lasting impact on the people that we bring to hear your voice.

Matthew:

It makes so much sense to me. You have a really simple way of talking to me. You are speaking very plainly. I love that.

God:

Yes, I speak plainly to you and to your readers. I want to be understood and known by your readers. I want to be your Friend, and I want to lead you from glory to glory. Be at peace. Bye for now.

Chapter 14
I Am Here

God:

Good morning, Matthew. How are you?

Matthew:

I am good. I am looking forward to hearing from you. I am really enjoying my times with you and hearing you speak to me. You have been so comforting to me in the things that you have been saying to me.

God:

Yes, I am glad that we have been having these times. It is good to talk to you and the readers. I am a God that doesn't want to be a mystery. I want people to know me and speak to me. I have a big heart of love that I want to share with people. You are my child, and the readers are my children. Doesn't every father want to speak to his children?

Matthew:

Yes, every father would like to speak to their children except in the most terrible situations. I am so glad that you are speaking to me, and you convinced me to write these books. It has become a real discipline to sit down each time and hear from you. It takes time and effort to sit down and type. But the good thing is that there will be a permanent record of what you have said to me. For this, I am grateful. If you hadn't given me the idea of writing this book, I would not have spoken to you as much as I am now.

God:

I am smart. I am a really wise God. I am speaking to you for your benefit and for that of your readers. I really do love you and love to speak to you clearly and simply. Why would I speak in hard language that is complicated for you to understand? Since you are a simple person with simple thinking, I speak to you in a simple language. If you were a theologian, I might use bigger words and more complex themes, but because you are simple, I speak in a way that is easy for you to understand.

Matthew:

You are all together wonderful to me.

God:

I am a God that wants to speak to my creation. I am a God that wants my creation to love me. I want my people to follow Jesus and come and draw close to me. I am in love with my people. I have so much for them to see and hear from me. I am right here, available to the people of God. I want to reach out to them and speak to them face to face like I spoke to Moses. I want my people to not just know **about** me, but to really **know** me. I want them to love me and come to me, and I want to be their comfort and their source.

I want to come off the pages in the Bible, right down into their houses and speak face to face with them. It says in John 14:23, "Jesus answered and said to him, 'If anyone loves Me, he will keep My word; and My Father will love him, and We will come to him and make Our home with him.' "

Matthew:

That is true. Yes, I have seen you in my house, and we have communicated with each other. It is comforting to know that scripturally, you can come and make your home with us. Many people read that passage and say that Jesus meant that the Holy Spirit would come and make his home with us. But the verse can be taken literally, and you can come to earth and meet with us face to face like you did with Moses. And because we are in the New Covenant with greater promises, we can know you and meet you.

Right now, I can see you in my kitchen as I type. I know the world would love to meet you.

God:

Yes, I have come to meet with you today. You are not only taking dictation of my words through your spirit, but you can also see me smiling at you in a vision. I want the people of God to know that you are not someone special and unique who has a greater access to me than they do. I want the readers to know that if they have faith, I can come to visit them also. I am not a God that is far off. I am a God that is right here. I am a God that wants to meet with my creation face to face. Jesus announced, "Blessed are the pure in heart, for they shall see God" (Matthew 5:8). It is therefore possible to see me and meet me and have fellowship with me. A person does not have to wait to go to heaven to meet me. They can know me, meet me and have a great time with me.

Matthew:

You fill me with such joy. Your ways are higher than mine. You are so full of surprises for me. You are a delight to me. I am so happy that you love and accept me. I did so many bad things in my life, yet through the blood of Jesus, you have washed me clean.

And now, you are in my house smiling at me as I type, and I don't want to shrink away from you. I know that I am loved and accepted and worthy in your sight.

God:

Yes, you are worthy of my love. I love you with all of my heart. I want all of my creation to be washed in Jesus' blood and forgiven so that they, too, can meet me and know me and feel comfortable and loved in my presence. I want to pour out my love on the world and for the world to want and embrace me.

Some people, who have not yet given their lives to me, will read this book. They are people that I love and who I want to draw to myself. I love everyone who is reading these words. I want to draw all men to myself.

Matthew:

I have often thought that people who are not Christians might read this book. I have wondered about making it simpler, but I guess you know what you are saying and what you are directing me to say. I encourage those readers to ask Jesus to come into their lives so that the Holy Spirit starts to speak to them and lead them. You have such a great heart, God. Thank you so much for loving me and sharing your heart with me.

God:

It is fun to speak to you. You are a great vessel to speak through. You are a good person to communicate with. You are my choice to bring this message to people. It is exciting to be speaking to you and for you to be able to realize as I speak that you already know of me. It is so refreshing to have the ability to speak without religious filters to the world. I am really enjoying myself, and I am glad that you are taking the time to write my messages. I would love it if all of the readers learned how to hear me speak to them. I want to speak to my creation one on one.

The next step for them all is to learn to hear from me and for them to start their own journals and let me speak to them personally. I have so much that I want to say and to show them. I am a God who is pregnant with things that I want to bring forth in the world through my people.

Matthew:

You bring me such joy. I can see that you have gone back to heaven now, but I loved seeing you in a vision. I love you so much. You bring me comfort and wisdom. Your words are a delight to me. Thank you for speaking to me and using me to write so that other people can hear you.

God:

It is a joyful thing for me to speak to you. I have been waiting for this for all of your life. You wrote the book, "Jesus Speaking Today," which was really good, and it has blessed quite a few people. You never knew that you would one day revisit that book and write more on the same subjects. So now, instead of one page with each post in that book, you are writing much more. In that book, Jesus spoke, and now, I am speaking. We have so many more words with much more depth and clarity. You never knew you were going to do this, but we knew, and we had everything planned.

Matthew:

Yes, you knew and had it all planned. I am so comfortable with you speaking on these subjects, and I am really glad that you are expanding on what Jesus said. This was such a good idea.

God:

Every one of my ideas is a good one. I am smart and intelligent. Man does not seem to know that yet. They seem to think that they are the smart and intelligent ones, but as the world becomes more depraved, people are going to search me out for answers. One day, all men will know who I am and whether or not they have accepted Jesus as their Lord, they will all bow to him.

Matthew:

I look forward to getting to know you better.

God:

Have a good day, Matthew. Have a good day, readers!

Chapter 15
Greater Works

God:

Hello, Matthew, how are you today?

Matthew:

I am really great. My books are doing well on Kindle, and I am very happy with the down loads. I have a book called "Finding Intimacy with Jesus made Simple" with a hundred downloads so far this month. It is a really good book with a lot of revelation in it about the life of Jesus, and I am so happy that a hundred people have bought it and are going to read it and be blessed by it.

God:

You are so easy to please.

Matthew:

I am. It makes my heart so glad that such a good book is being read by so many people. It is as though I am reaching through the book and transforming them. You said that we will do greater works then you. I am so happy because if those hundred people really meditate on that book, it really will help them to grow close to Jesus. My heart is full of joy. You are so good to me. You encouraged me to write, and now I have touched 700 lives this month with my books. I am just so glad. Only 120 people were in the upper room when your Spirit fell in Acts, yet this month, I have had 700 people read my books. You are the great and mighty God who makes me achieve exceedingly and abundantly more than I can even think or pray (Ephesians 3:20).

God:

Yes, I am a God that can help you do things that are amazing and more than you can ever think or dream. To think that one of your books is outselling Joyce Meyers "Battlefield of the Mind." Every time that you check the status of that book, and you see yourself outselling such a popular speaker, your heart is filled with joy. I am a God that lights up your heart and propels you toward success. I am a God that can see people achieve more than my Son ever did.

I am a God that lights up the hearts of people and motivates them to do great things with the power of the Holy Spirit working within them. I am a God that displays his glory through the lives of ordinary people. I am the God that takes a normal person and makes them great. And when I glorify a normal person, I help to glorify my name in the world. I have a great future for every person who grasps that I have created them for good things and who pursues those things through the power of the Holy Spirit.

Matthew:

I am so happy that you work in my life. That book, originally called, "Kingdom Nuggets," is doing so much better with the new title, "Finding Intimacy with Jesus Made Simple." My friend, Praying Medic, as he is known on the internet, said that book sales really depend heavily on the title of a book and the cover design. So I changed the title and the book's cover, and now, it is doing really well.

I am so touched that you used Praying Medic to help me change my mind and lead me into action when it came to that book because so many people are ordering it now. All glory and honor go to your Holy Spirit for leading me to make that change. You are a wonderful Guide in my life. It didn't cost much to republish the book with the new title and the new cover, and now, so many more people are being blessed because of that decision.

God:

One of the keys to doing great works is to have a heart that is open to the leading of the Holy Spirit. You could have been obstinate and believed that your title and the cover for the book were just fine, and you would not have made the change. But because you were open to the leading of the Holy Spirit, you have seen the success of the book with the new title and cover.

We speak to people all the time, and they tend to ignore us and dismiss the thought as "crazy," thinking that they just made it up themselves. But when people heed our words and act on them, then good things happen. We can really use many people to do different things. We can use every person in a radical way, and every person on earth can learn to do greater works.

Some people might read that and scoff at it, but most people can lead more than 120 people to a new relationship with Christ. With just $120, people could give your book as a gift to 120 other people. They can radically change the life of another person since your book is 99 cents to buy. People can really have a great effect on others if they just deny themselves and lay down their life and are willing to be led by the Holy Spirit. Simply sharing this book on Facebook or sending 10 people a gift on Kindle would change lives. I can do great things through every person if they would only lay down their lives and submit to the leading of the Holy Spirit.

Matthew:

That is really a key — to deny oneself and lay down their life for you. Sometimes, that takes a lot of preaching and a lot of messages to achieve in a person's life. Wouldn't the world be in a good place if all of the Christians were led by your Spirit?

God:

I long to have a people that not only hear my voice but march to the beat of my heart. I long for a people that can hear me and obey me. I have so much that I could do with the world if the people of God could simply hear me speaking for themselves without a book like this. I have so much for the common folk. I have so much to share from my heart with the ordinary person.

I am saddened by the fact that many Christians can't hear me. I want to speak and share my heart. I want to lead my people to do greater works than my Son. I have so much to share and so many good ideas that will work. I have so many good things that people can do. I have the keys to life and the personal keys to the success of every individual. You don't need to read a book on how to succeed; you simply need to be able to hear from me and be led by me. That is what makes you such a key person in the Kingdom, Matthew. You can hear us, and you follow us. We lead you and direct you in all that you do. You are a joy to us. You may be a little person in the Kingdom now, and not many people know you. But just like Joseph was in the prison unknown by all except the head jailer that put him in charge, he still came to a time in life that he was placed as second in charge of Egypt. So, too, you will come out of obscurity into the light and favor of men. I have your whole life planned, and one day, many people will know who you are.

Matthew:

Thank you, Lord. Thank you for your promises in my life. I thank you for the life that I live. I thank you that I can speak into the lives of 700 people this month through my books. I am really enjoying my life and working on three books at a time. I thank you for the prophecy site that earns income to produce my books. I thank you for the favor on my life. I thank you for every part of my life. I even thank you for the suffering because I know through that, I grow in character and compassion for others. I thank you that I am exceeding the expectations of my teachers at school. I thank you for the way that you lead me and that you are leading me to impact the nations. I thank you for the life that I am currently living and the life that you have planned for me in the future. It is my prayer that my life brings you glory.

God:

You do bring me glory, Matthew. You are so real and transparent. People love your heart and the way that you express yourself. You have learned to speak with authority and with honesty to the people. You are a treasure to the Kingdom of God. You exceed the expectations of the world. You are a real surprise, and you are an inspiration to many people. You cope with so much; you overcome so much, and no matter what comes against you, you seem to press through and conquer every single attack. You make us look good. I am so happy to be your friend. You are such a joy to us.

Matthew:

Your words really touch me and bless me deeply. I enjoy speaking to you. Yes, I am going to live to bring you a lot of glory. My life will testify to the power and strength of your Holy Spirit. I live to bring honor to your name.

God:

It was a joy to speak to you today. Time to proofread this and post it.

Closing Thoughts

You might have read this book and been wondering how you can have a relationship with God like I do. You might be wishing that God would speak to you as clearly as he speaks to me. I want to encourage you, not to read books like this simply to know that God speaks today, but I want to encourage you to start to speak to God for yourself and draw near to him yourself.

I am no one special. God wants to speak to all of us as clearly as he has spoken in this book. I suggest two books for you to read so that you can hear from God for yourself.

The first book is called "How to Hear from God Easily" by Adam Houge.

The second book is called "Hearing God's Voice Made Simple" by Praying Medic.

You have a choice. You can be a Christian that depends on others to hear a message from God and to be taught by him or you can go to him yourself and have him speak to you personally. I encourage you to seek God. Sure, you can watch for the next four books in this series as I write them, but I encourage you to start to hear from him way before then.

God wants to speak to you, and he wants to lead you into a prosperous life full of meaning and fulfillment. He is your God, and he is the One that wants to lead and sustain you. I encourage you to get to know him by learning to hear from him.

I'd love to hear from you.

One way that you can bless me as a writer is by writing an honest and candid review of my book on Amazon. I always read the reviews of my books, and I would love to hear what you have to say about this one.

Before I buy a book, I read the reviews first. You can make a good decision about a book when you have read enough honest reviews from readers. One good way to make sure this book sells well and to give me positive feedback is by writing a review for me. It doesn't cost you a thing but helps me enormously and the future readers of this book.

To sow into my book writing ministry, to read my blog or to request your own personal prophecy from God, you can visit http://personal-prophecy-today.com. All of your gifts will go toward the books that I write and self-publish.

To write to me about this book or any other thoughts, please feel free to contact me at my personal email address at survivors.sanctuary@gmail.com.

You can also friend request me at Facebook at Matthew Robert Payne. Please send me a message if we have no friends in common as a lot of scammers now send me friend requests.

You can also do me a huge favor and share this book on Facebook as a recommended book to read. This will help me and other readers.

How to Sponsor a Book Project

If you have been blessed by this book, you might consider sponsoring a book for me. It normally costs me between fifteen hundred and two thousand dollars or more to produce each book that I write, depending on the length of the book.

If you seek the Holy Spirit about financing a book for me, I know that the Lord would be eternally grateful to you. Consider how much this book has blessed you and then think of hundreds or even thousands of people who would be blessed by a book of mine. As you are probably aware, the vast majority of my books are ninety-nine cents on Kindle, which proves to you that book writing is indeed a ministry for me and not a money- making venture. I would be very happy if you supported me in this.

If you have any questions for me or if you want to know what projects I am currently working on that your money might finance, you can write to me at survivors.sanctuary@gmail.com and ask me for more information. I would be pleased to give you more details about my projects. You can sow any amount to my ministry by simply sending me money via the PayPal link at this address: http://personal-prophecy-today.com/support-my-ministry/ You can be sure that your support, no matter the amount, will be used for the publishing of helpful Christian books for people to read.

Other Books by Matthew Robert Payne

The Parables of Jesus Made Simple

The Prophetic Supernatural Experience

Prophetic Evangelism Made Simple

Your Identity in Christ

His Redeeming Love- A Memoir

Writing and Self-Publishing Christian Nonfiction

Coping with your Pain and Suffering

Living for Eternity

Jesus Speaking Today

Great Cloud of Witnesses Speak

My Radical Encounters with Angels

Finding Intimacy with Jesus Made Simple

My Radical Encounters with Angels- Book Two

A Beginner's Guide to the Prophetic

Michael Jackson Speaks from Heaven

Coming Soon:

7 Keys to Intimacy with Jesus

Go into All the World

You can find my published books on my Amazon author page here: http://tinyurl.com/jq3h893

About the Author

Matthew was raised in a Baptist church and was led to the Lord at the tender age of 8 years old. Matthew has experienced some pain and darkness in his life, and this has led him to have a deep compassion and love for all people.

Today, he runs two Facebook groups, one called "Open Heavens and Intimacy with Jesus" and one called "Prophetic Training Group." Matthew has a commission from the Lord to train up prophets and to mentor others in the Christian faith. He does this through his groups and by writing relevant books for the Christian faith.

God has commissioned him to write 50 books in his life, and he spends his days writing and earning the money to self-publish. You can support him by donating money at http://personal-prophecy-today.com or by requesting your own personal prophecy.

It is Matthew's prayer that this book has blessed you, and he hopes it will lead you into a deeper and more intimate relationship with God.

9 781684 110438